NATIONA
GEOGRAP

The Sun

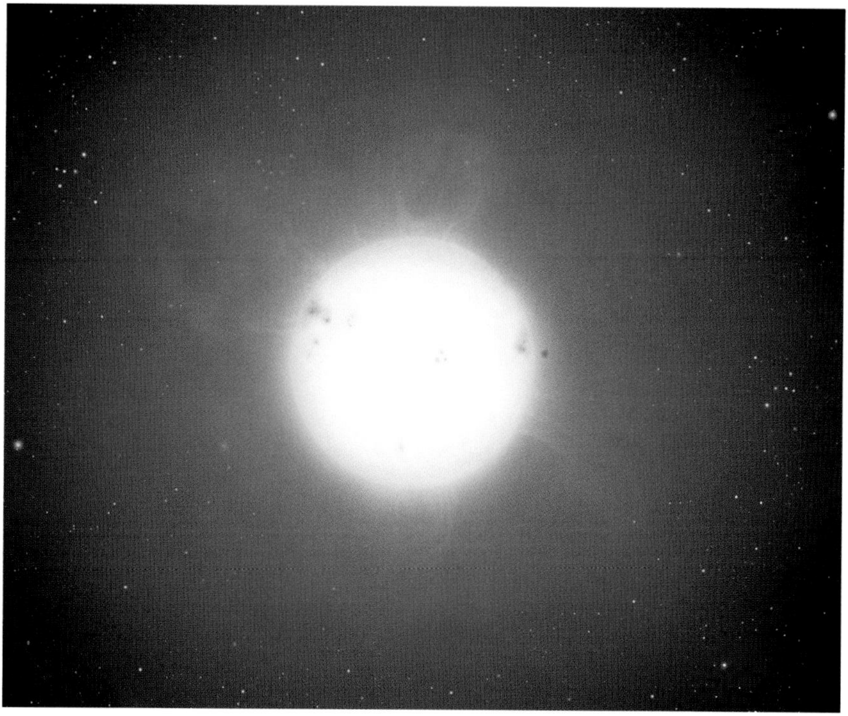

Anita Garmon

Contents

Introduction

Most days we wake up to see the sun shining in the sky. We feel its warmth. We enjoy the light it shines on us. We miss the sun when clouds cover the sky.

But what is the sun? Where did it come from? How did it get into the sky?

Long ago, people knew little about the sun. They did not know why it suddenly appeared in the morning. They did not know where it went at night. They made up stories to explain what was happening in the sky each day and night.

Sun Tales from Long Ago

An Inuit Tale

The Inuit people live in Greenland, an island country in the cold northern Atlantic Ocean. The Inuits told this tale long ago.

The moon god and the sun god were brother and sister. One day, they got into a terrible fight. The sun god spread dark grease all over her brother's face. Afraid of what her brother might do, she ran away as far as she could into the sky. Her brother chased after her. And every day, the chase goes on. That is why the sun shares the sky with moon.

A Greek Tale

The **ancient** Greeks believed that there was a sun god, Helios. Each day he drove his golden chariot across the sky. He started from his palace in the east and drove to his palace in the west. As he traveled during the day, his golden helmet shined brightly and light came from his chest. At night, he sailed back in a ferry boat to his palace in the east.

An Inca Tale

The Inca lived in South America hundreds of years ago. They called the sun *Inti*, which means "light." They believed that the sun went into the ocean each night. After swimming all night, the sun woke up refreshed and rose to the sky.

What Is the Sun?

Today we know that the sun is a star. The sun looks much bigger and brighter than other stars because it is much closer to us than other stars. Even though it's the nearest star, the sun is over 90 million miles (150 million kilometers) away. That's like traveling around the Earth almost 4,000 times!

Like all stars, the sun is a great big ball of burning gases. It looks round and solid. But it is actually boiling and bubbling and always changing.

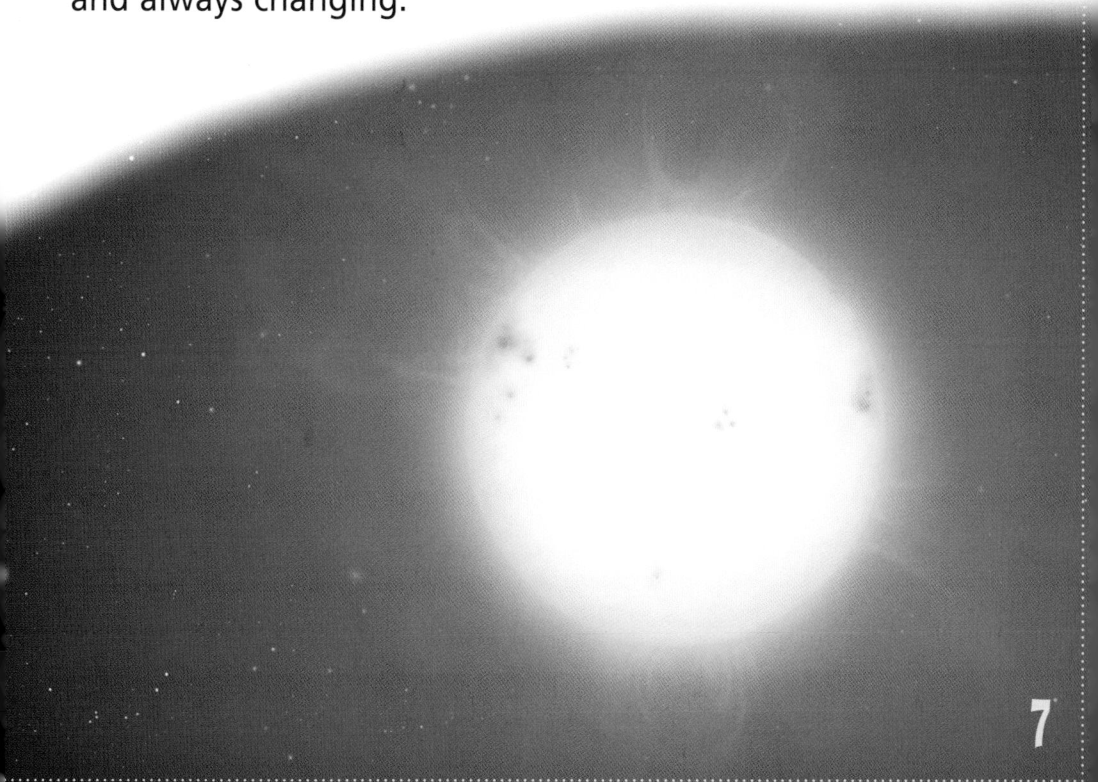

We know the sun is very hot because we can feel its heat from far away. Scientists can figure out the **temperature** of a star from its color. They have found out that the temperature on the surface of the sun is about 10,000° F (5,500° C). That's 20 times hotter than a pizza oven!

The sun is even hotter at its center. Its temperature can rise as high as 27 million° F (15 million° C). That's 50,000 times hotter than a pizza oven!

Scientists think the sun is 4.6 billion years old. They believe that it will keep on shining for another 5 billion years. Then it will start to die. It will fade and shrink to a dark ball of cinders not much bigger than Earth.

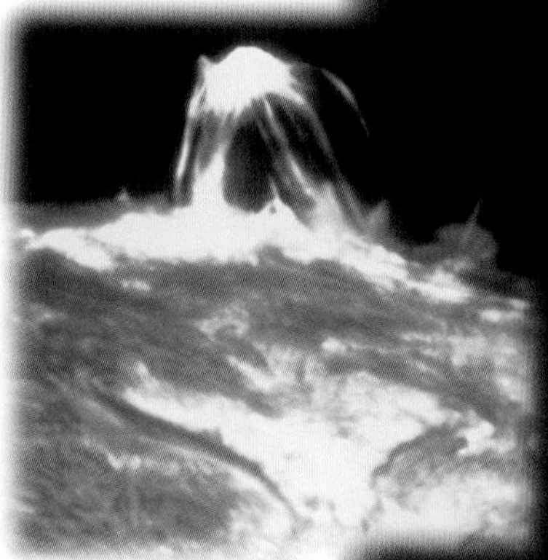

The sun gives off light and heat. Only a ► tiny bit of the sun's light and heat reaches Earth. The rest goes into space.

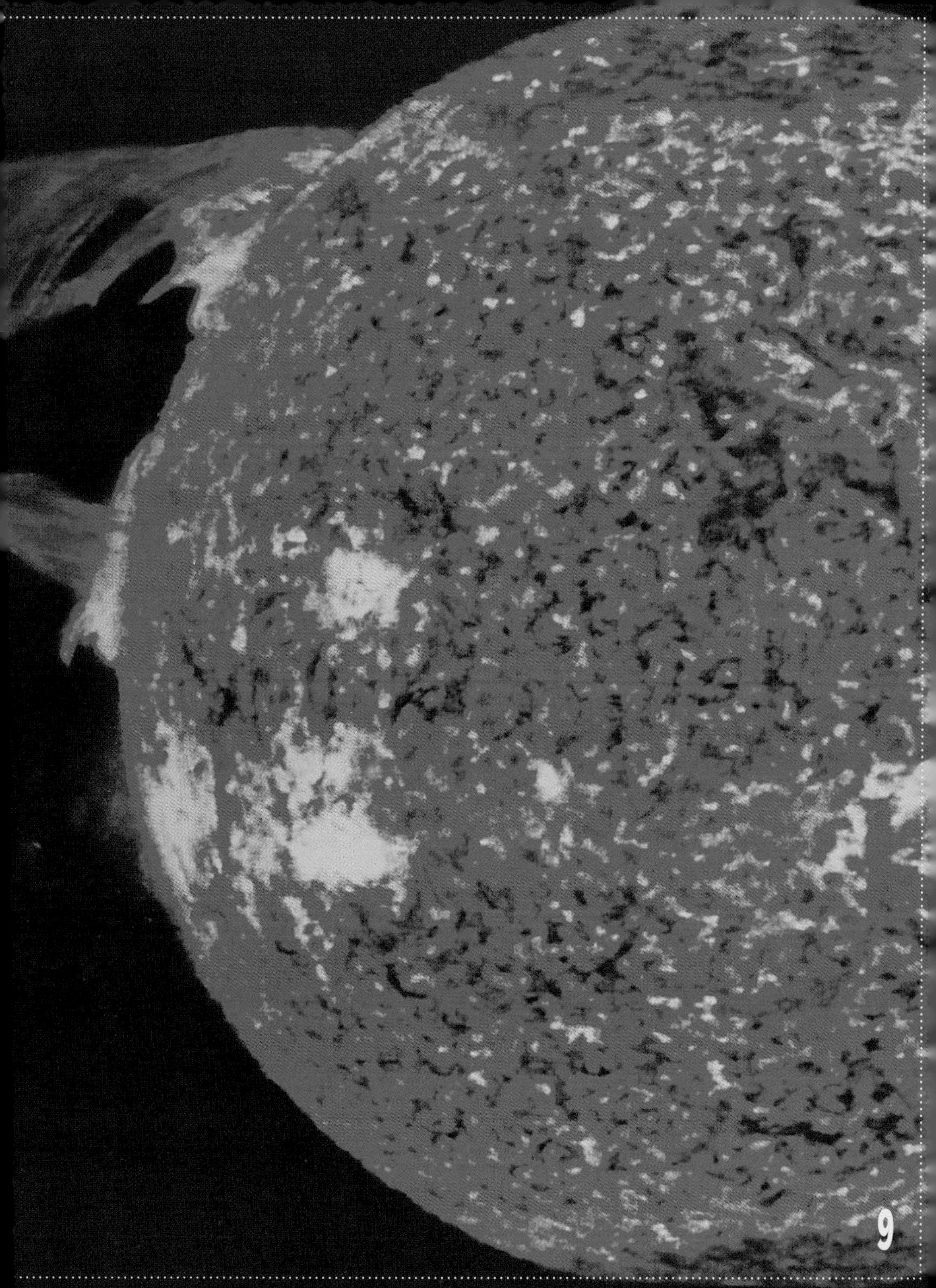

Our Solar System

The Earth is just one of the bodies that circle around the sun. We call this group of **planets** and other bodies that circle the sun the **solar system**. The sun is at the center of the solar system. The word *solar* comes from the Latin word for the sun, *sol*.

There are nine planets in the solar system. They travel around the sun in paths called **orbits**. Earth is the third closest planet to the sun. The planets Mercury and Venus are closer to the sun than Earth is. The planets Mars, Jupiter, Saturn, Uranus, Neptune, and Pluto are all farther from the sun than Earth is.

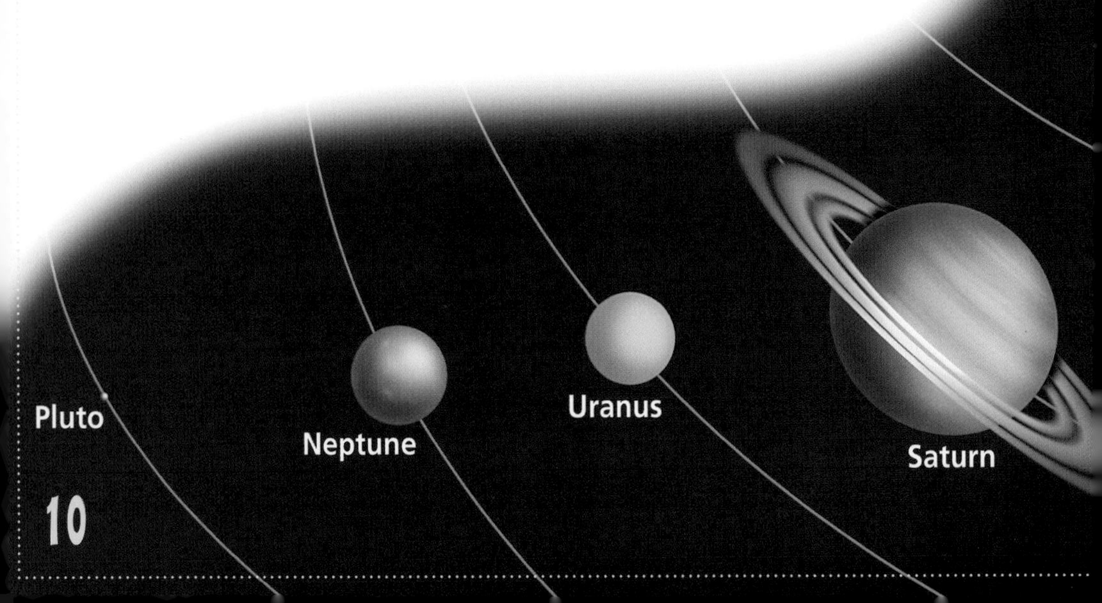

The planets close to the sun are much warmer than the planets far away from the sun. Mercury is the warmest planet and Pluto is the coldest. The Earth's distance from the sun keeps it at just the right temperature for living things.

▼ The planets in our solar system travel around the sun.

Why Is the Sun Important?

Without the sun, there would be no life on Earth. The Earth would be a cold, black rock in space. Light and heat from the sun allow the Earth to be home to millions of living things.

Heat from the sun warms the Earth. Plants and animals need temperatures that are not too hot or too cold. The sun gives the Earth the right amount of heat to keep temperatures comfortable for plants and animals. If the Earth were closer to the sun, temperatures would be too hot for life. If it were farther away from the sun, temperatures would be too cold.

Plants and animals need food to live and grow. Green plants soak up the sun's light and turn it into food. Then animals eat the plants to get the food they need to live and grow.

What Causes Day and Night?

The sun also gives the Earth day and night. Every morning, the sun rises in the east. The sky becomes light, and day begins. The sun climbs higher in the sky until it reaches its highest point at noon.

In the afternoon, the sun sinks lower in the sky. At sunset, the sun drops out of sight in the west. The sky darkens, and night begins.

It looks as if the sun is traveling across the sky. But it is actually the Earth that is moving, not the sun. The Earth is **rotating**, or spinning like a top. It takes one day, or 24 hours, for the Earth to rotate once around.

The sun always shines, but it lights only half of the Earth at a time. The other half is dark. As the Earth rotates, different parts of the planet face the sun. When the part of the Earth where you live faces the sun, it is daytime. When your part of the Earth turns away from the sun, it is night. When you are eating lunch, what do you think people on the other side of the Earth are doing?

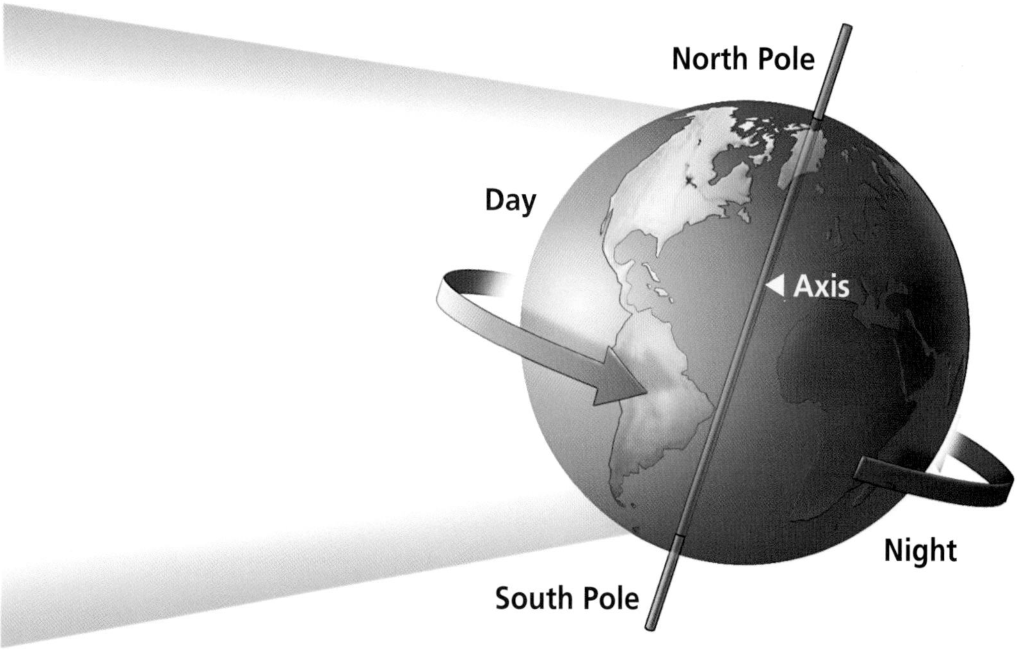

▲ The Earth spins on an imaginary line through its center. This line is called an axis. It goes from the North Pole to the South Pole.

What Causes the Seasons?

The sun also causes the **seasons**. In most parts of the Earth, the number of daylight hours changes with the seasons. The days start to get longer in the spring. When summer comes there are many hours of sunlight and the sun is high in the sky. When fall arrives, the days grow shorter. Winter has the shortest days of all.

▲ Summer

▲ Spring

▼ Winter

▲ Fall

The Earth **revolves** around, or orbits, the sun. It takes a full year for the Earth to revolve around the sun. The Earth has seasons because its **axis** is tilted. The Earth always leans in the same direction as it revolves around the sun.

Look at the drawing. You can see that different parts of the Earth lean toward the sun as the Earth spins around it. The amount of sunlight hitting the northern and southern parts of the Earth changes depending on where the Earth is in its yearly orbit. This causes the seasons to change.

When it is winter where you live, your part of the Earth is tilted away from the sun. So, you get less light and heat. During summer, your part of the Earth is tilted toward the sun. You get more light and heat.

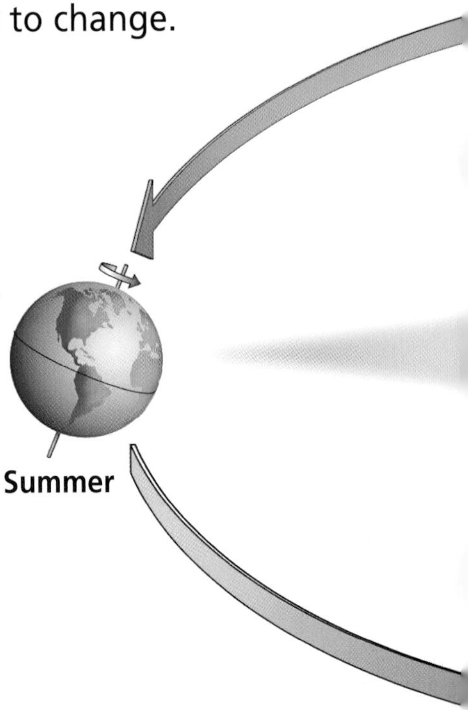

It takes the Earth 365¼ days, or a year, ▲ to revolve around the sun.

There is an imaginary line across the middle of the Earth called the **Equator**. It separates the northern part of the Earth from the southern part. When it is summer in the northern part of the Earth, it is winter in the southern part. That's why it is winter in North America when it is summer in Australia.

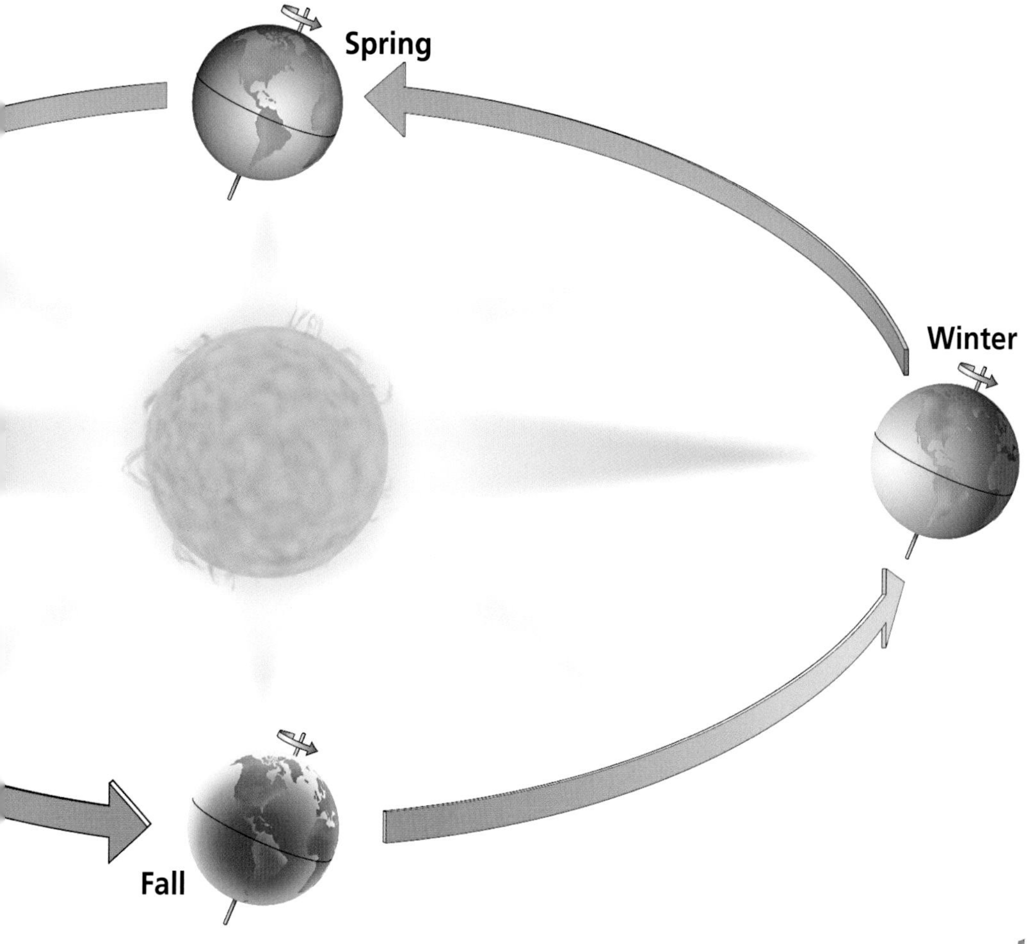

Studying the Sun

We know much more than we used to about the sun. But there is still a lot to learn. Scientists continue to study the sun in many ways.

Scientists have built special **telescopes** to look at the sun. They are called solar telescopes. They are built to protect people's eyes from the blinding rays of the sun. You should never look at the sun directly. The rays can hurt your eyes or even blind you.

▼ The McMath-Pierce Solar Telescope is the world's largest solar telescope.

Scientists also study the sun from space. They have sent solar telescopes into space. These telescopes send pictures of the sun back to Earth. The pictures show parts of the sun that no one has ever seen before. There are many mysteries about the sun that scientists have yet to discover.

▲ The space station Skylab carried telescopes to observe the sun.

Sun Facts

Average Distance from Earth
93 million miles
(150 million kilometers)

Temperature at the Surface
10,000° F (5,500° C)

Temperature at the Center
27 million° F (15 million° C)

Age
4.6 billion years

Glossary

ancient	very old; having existed long ago
axis	an imaginary line that the Earth rotates around
Equator	an imaginary line that runs around the middle of Earth and separates the northern and southern halves of the planet
orbit	the path of one object around another
planet	a large body that orbits a star
revolve	to move in a circular orbit around an object
rotate	to spin on an axis
seasons	periods of the year, such as spring, summer, fall, and winter
solar system	the sun and the planets, moons, and other bodies that orbit the sun
star	a ball of burning gases in space that looks like a bright spot in the night sky
telescope	an instrument that makes distant objects appear larger
temperature	how hot something is

Index